My CRIES *of* YESTERDAY

ANGELICA GALBRAITH

Fulton Books, Inc.
Meadville, PA

Published by Fulton Books 2020

ISBN 978-1-64654-489-9 (paperback)
ISBN 978-1-64654-851-4 (hardcover)
ISBN 978-1-64654-490-5 (digital)

Printed in the United States of America

I would like to dedicate this book to my brothers. Our lives haven't always been that easy, but our future has turned out better than anyone would have thought. My desire to write this book was difficult, but I finally did it, and there will be many more to come.

CONTENTS

ACKNOWLEDGMENTS

I wish to thank my Lord Jesus Christ. Without you in my heart, I wouldn't have been pushed to write this book. To the best husband in the world, I love you and thank you for being by my side. To my children, nothing is impossible, and I love you. To my mother, Christina Ramos Zamora, thank you for changing and being a better mom. To my brothers, Jerry Zamora Jr. and Jeffrey Lee Zamora, and my sister-in-law, Veronica Zamora, you guys are my world. I love you all so much. To my best friend, Erika Rubio, whom I call sister, thank you for always being there through thick and thin. You are the best sister I could ever have. And to those who have hurt me, without you, I would not be the strong woman I am today.

PART ONE

Innocence Taken

So do not fear, for I am with you; do not be dismayed, for I am your God. I will strengthen you and help you; I will uphold you with my righteous right hand.

—Isaiah 41:10

CHAPTER ONE

Not a Home

Waking up in the middle of the night with loud screams had
become routine at the age of five. My little brother was always
having nightmares. At first, I thought it was a joke because his eyes
were always open. I was afraid of my brother, but I also had this tre-
mendous feeling of sadness in my heart that would bring tears to my
eyes as I would watch him kick and scream while pinning himself to
a corner. I'd ask myself, *Why is my brother this way?*

It was very hard to see him that way every night. My mother
would run to our room and try to wake him, but she wasn't always
successful, so then she would hold him in her arms until he would
fall back to sleep. I would lie back down next to him and look out the
window just to stare at the moon. I would see two eyes and a smile
and then shut my eyes, feeling as if it were telling me everything was
going to be okay. Our mornings always started off with the smell of
breakfast and music playing. I would get up from my bed slowly,
trying not to wake up my little brother from being up all night, run
down the stairs while my parents were talking in the kitchen, and
jump into my father's arms. As the Spanish music would play, he
would start dancing with me in his arms. I felt like the princess in
the books my mother would read to me. I was the happiest kid at
that moment.

My father was a very aggressive person who drank too much
and wasn't always working. He would have his friends over at times,

and all they ever did was get drunk, sing, and dance. My father came from a family of musicians, so the singing and dancing ran in our blood. My mother was great at maintaining our home and taking care of us. She dealt with a lot of abuse from my father. She was a woman who didn't really have a mother to show her how to take care of herself. Her mother passed away when she was six, which led to my mother's lack of a parent's love. Things with our parents weren't always ordinary. I never saw my parents being affectionate. In the seventies, if you were having a child, you basically just get married, so it was what I call a had-to relationship.

One day, my mother was getting us ready to go to a party. She was pregnant at the time. I was going to have another little brother. I didn't know how far along she was, but I did know she was showing. We left for the party, and my father stayed behind, drinking. When the party was almost over, my mother decided it was time to leave because it was getting dark. We got into the car to head back home. My mother got us down and started walking down the walkway to get to the front door. I was holding my brother by the hand, walking toward her, and saw that she had this blank stare while looking at the front two windows that were open.

We had no curtains but this light-brown shade that you could pull down to cover the window, so you could definitely see a silhouette at night if the lights were on. Our stairway started at one of those windows, and we only had one bathroom, which was upstairs. We heard someone coming down, and it was very obvious that it was a woman who was wearing heels.

Next thing I know, my mother was banging on the door, yelling, but no one was answering. I started getting angry, and my mother started heading toward the back door. I told my brother, "Sit on the porch, and I'll be right back." I started walking behind her, and I saw this woman coming out the back door and my dad just standing there with a smile on his face as if it were all a joke. My mother tried to grab her, but my father stopped her, and the other woman walked away.

I was so angry and had so many questions: Why was my father acting this way? Who was this woman? Why was she in our home?

in our bathroom? in our bedroom? Was she in my room? My mother was crying as she walked inside, and I ran back to my brother. She opened the front door and told us to get inside.

I felt this unsafe feeling walking in. I knew there was going to be a fight, and when that happened, it was my mother who always took the hits. "Go upstairs," she said. And I heard her yell, "I want a divorce!" My brother and I walk into our room, and I looked around as if that woman had taken something from our rooms and bathroom. Now that I think of it, I must have looked hilarious walking into every room as if we had just gotten robbed.

My brother was so traumatized by all the fighting that went on that he just went straight to his corner of the bed. As we lay next to each other for comfort, I looked out the window to the moon as I always did. The nights we were in bed and our parents were fighting were scary. The moon that once smiled at me was now angry. It had me imagining the Wicked Witch in *The Wizard of Oz* was coming for us.

My attention was stuck on the window because I had to protect my brother from her, and I couldn't sleep much those nights. Time went by, and I suddenly heard a door slam and heard my grandfather's voice. I ran downstairs to greet him, and he gave me a kiss and a hug.

"Let's sit down and talk," said my grandfather. "What are you going to do about all this?"

And my mother said, "Divorce."

I saw my dad take his wallet out and throw it at my grandfather's chest. He then said, "She can have all my money!" My father started walking up the stairs and came back down with all his clothes. I cried and begged him to not leave. He kissed me and left. I didn't see much of my dad after that. He went on to live with the woman whom we saw in our home, and they had two children.

My mother went on with her life alone for a while and had my new baby brother. I remember being outside the hospital window with my father and Jerry to take a look at my new baby brother. My mother named him Jeffrey. I was pretty excited for him to come home. I helped my mother a lot with whatever she needed for him.

Things were okay for a bit, except for that empty feeling I had of my father not being home. She then met a new man who had no children and was never married. Everything took a turn for the worst when we finally met him.

CHAPTER TWO

A Monster

The phone rang.

"Hello?" The person on the other line started asking me questions about my mother. I was quickly angered by this disgusting man who was asking me perverted questions about her. I hang up and went about playing with my brothers. Not long before that, we saw a man who started coming into our home, hugging and kissing our mother.

He was touching her in ways that were inappropriate, especially in front of us. It led me to believe he was the one who was calling with all the dirty questions. I despised him so much. The only man who should have been there should be my father. There was a lot after that I don't remember, until one night, I woke up to my brother Jerry's crying. It wasn't the nightmare cry; it was a different cry. I always slept with my brothers in the same bed and was a light sleeper. That night, I turned over, and the man (who had moved in) was hitting my brother in the head, asking him who his father was.

My brother would say "Jerry is my dad," and he would hit him harder. My brother realized he needed to say this man's name. They called him Rocky. Our monster was dark with ugly teeth and tattoos all over his body. One tattoo in particular that I would always remember was one on his neck of a skull with a syringe. My brother would yell out his name, and then he would stop and go back to my mother's room. I cried for my little brother and had so much hate toward this man. My mother came into the room and asked if we were okay, and I yelled out, "No! He hit Jerry really hard!"

My mom went back to their room, and I heard an argument, then it got quiet. Next thing I know, he was walking into our room and came and hit me on the head. My head was throbbing, but I also felt numb. I was so scared of this man that I just took the pain and stayed awake, hoping he wouldn't come into the room again. After that incident, I don't remember us getting hit again for a while.

One night, my mother woke us and told us to stay in the room and not go downstairs. She went downstairs for a bit. Now that I am older, I'm assuming she was locking all windows and doors. My mother came back upstairs, looked out our window that was always open, (we never had air-conditioning) and started yelling to someone, saying, "He's not here! Just go away!" Our bed was always at the window, so I got up to look out, and it looked like my cousin Beto and a gang of guys with bats and pipes. Next thing I know, I heard windows breaking downstairs. We started crying and screaming, and I heard my mom yell that she was going to call the police. Next thing I know, I was waking up my mother's cousin Connie, who lived across from us, and she took us in for the night.

On the next day, I realized that we were moving out and moving in with my aunt Lydia, but everyone called her Lila. I was actually excited because my cousin Becky and I were close just like my mother and aunt, and we were going to get to spend a lot of time together. I didn't see Rocky around for a while, but I did see my dad a little more. My mother would walk me to school and pick me up every day. I loved school; I loved reading in class and writing.

Coming home one day, I walked into my aunt's apartment and saw Rocky there talking to one of my uncles. I felt the anger again, and this time, it was toward my mother as well for having him there after everything he did to me and my little brother. Rocky was a man who, from what I know now, owed people money, shot up heroin, drank every day, worked as a carpenter on occasion, and had been in the service before. He came toward me and said, "Hi, mija." And I just ran upstairs. I had to make sure my brothers were okay.

My aunt lived in the same projects as we did, just on another street. They were all green with beige trim, and they all looked pretty much the same inside. As I was upstairs, I wondered if my mother was still seeing him, so I went back downstairs slowly and saw them hugging. Both my brothers were safe playing with their toys. I was so upset I threw a tantrum, hoping it would make him leave, but it didn't work. He tried to be nice, but deep down, I knew it was fake. I noticed that he was coming around a lot more; he was at every barbecue or birthday parties we would have. He was always pretty much drunk at those events.

One morning, I woke up and saw my mom packing all our things. She looked up and said, "We are moving into a house." Yay! I started waking Jerry up to tell him the good news. "We're moving in with Rocky" she said.

I was devasted and scared. "I do not want to go," I said.

She yelled at me and said I had to. So we moved pretty quick into our first house on San Jacinto Street. The house was big and had a huge yard with a fence around it. It was blue and white, had two bedrooms, and was painted all white inside. There was also another very small house in the same lot that the landlord was using for storage. So you can imagine how big the yard was.

We settled in, and things started going okay for a while, until one day, he got home from work and started fighting with my mom and punched her in the face. We sat on the couch. We were so frightened of him that we didn't make a sound or even move. My mom would just take his hits as if she were used to it.

My mom found a job at this hotel called Christy Estates; it was a very popular place that many people wanted to stay in. A few of them had custom-made Jacuzzis that were very beautiful. At times, she would have me go on the weekends to help her. It made me wonder at times if she took me so he wouldn't be near me. I liked helping her, but I found myself always worried about my brothers. Rocky didn't always work and stayed home with us. My brothers and I shared a room, so if we weren't in there, we were outside. We couldn't stand being in the living room even to watch TV. We walked around on eggshells every single minute we were around him.

There was a particular day that I remember and wish had never happened. Rocky yelled at my brother Jerry and told him to go inside to take a shower. It was as if he would just get angry for no reason and take it out on us. My brother had that terrifying look on his face going into the bathroom while Rocky was right behind him. Jeffrey and I sat on the couch and turned the TV on. I started hearing Jerry screaming, and it sounded as if he were getting thrown around from wall to wall like a rag doll. I started crying and got up and went outside to look for something, anything that I could use to kill him. I had these thoughts for so long. I had had enough! There was so much hate and pain in my heart. If we had owned a gun in that house, I would have killed him without a doubt. I couldn't find anything that would hurt him. I walked back into the house and sat on the couch, then they finally came out of the bathroom. My brother's eye was closed shut with the biggest black eye I had ever seen. I was so mad but was also scared to death.

My mother got home. "What the hell happened?" she asked. Rocky sure did blame it on Jeffrey, who had no part in it. I know she must have known it was Rocky. She knew Jeffrey couldn't do something like that with his small hands. That black eye looked just like the ones she received from Rocky.

Why didn't my mother do anything? Why was Jeffrey in trouble? He did nothing wrong! I would have preferred my brothers and I to live anywhere else than at home. It was not okay to get a beating from Rocky whenever he felt like it. It was as if my brothers got the worst if he was drunk, and when he would shoot up heroin, I was the one who got the worst of it.

One day, I woke up with a fever and couldn't go to school, so my mother told me to just stay home. I didn't want to be alone with Rocky while she was away at work, but I was throwing up and very sick. I locked the door to our room as soon as my brothers and mother left the house.

"Open the door!" he yelled out. I didn't answer and was pretending to be asleep. He then kicked the door open and started yelling and cussing at me. I then felt his fists hitting me hard all over my back. He turned me around and pulled my shorts off and said, "This is what happens when you don't listen." I started screaming, and he put his hand over my mouth. He was so strong I couldn't move at all. I was being raped by this monster who was so evil. "If you ever say anything, I am going to break your mother's neck and kill your brothers," he said.

It was the worst pain I had ever felt at the age of ten. I really thought he was going to kill me. He punched me in the head and was done. He left the room, and I couldn't move. It hurt so bad I passed out. When I woke up, it felt like I had been asleep for so long. I figured my mom would be home by now. I started calling out, "Mom!" There was no answer.

Rocky came to my room. "She's not here yet. It's too early. Get your ass up," he said, laughing. "Get up and clean all that blood off." I was trying to sit up and couldn't. He grabbed me by one arm and dragged me to the bathroom and threw me into the tub and turned on the cold water. I was crying and screaming so hard, hoping someone would come to my rescue, but no one came. How could this monster do this to an innocent ten-year-old? I passed out again.

I woke up and heard voices talking to him in the living room right outside the bathroom, so I started to force myself to get up, grab the rag, and wash all the blood off my body gently. When I was done, I was able to stand up very slowly in the tub and managed to get out of the tub and put a towel around my body. I sat on the toilet for a while; my legs hurt so bad. The voices stopped, and I started to worry he would come in, so I walked out of the bathroom slowly, and he was there on the couch watching TV and drinking beer as if nothing happened. Not a word was said. I walked so slow it seemed like forever to get to my room. As I walk in, I noticed the sheets were gone. I got some clothes together and dressed myself slowly. Every inch of my body was in so much pain that I didn't even brush my hair and just laid in the bed and passed out.

CHAPTER THREE

Motherly Love?

The door slammed, and I awoke, feeling frightened. I knew my mom was home, and I was certain a fight was going to start, but I didn't hear yelling. Everyone who knew my mother knew she was just a loud person. She came into my room, and she saw that something wasn't right. I heard my mother asking him what was in the washer, and he told her he had to put in the sheets because I kept throwing up.

She walked into my room and asked if I was still throwing up. I didn't respond. As I faced the wall away from the door, she tapped my shoulder as if she thought I were asleep.

"No!" I yelled out in a mean way.

"Why are you mad?" she asked.

"I never want to stay here with him again."

She never asked me why or anything. "You and your brothers have to stay here with him when I am at work," she said. "You and your brothers will be here alone when he does work." My mother walked out, and I heard her in the kitchen, preparing for dinner and finishing the laundry.

I was hoping the blood on the sheets were still there so she could see what that bastard of a man had done to me. But I never heard a word. I stayed in my room the whole time and didn't come out. My brothers got home from school and went outside to play. We never asked each other questions or talked about the abuse. It was always bottled up. We never knew when something would trigger Rocky, and he would come for one of us.

"Come inside and eat dinner!" Rocky yelled out to my brothers. I heard his footsteps coming my way. "You're sick, so you won't eat dinner. You'll just throw it up," he said. I just fell asleep until I heard a dish break.

I heard him calling my mother names, and then I heard a slap. I heard my brothers playing outside, so I didn't worry. As for my mother, I was upset and just told myself, *She chose a man like him over us, so maybe it's what she wanted.* If there was ever something wrong that she said, he would hit her right away.

The next morning, my mother came into the room and told us to get up for school. My whole body was still in pain, but I was not about to stay home again with that bastard. I forced myself to get up and walk to the bathroom to brush my teeth as if nothing hurt so I wouldn't get questioned.

My mother wouldn't cook us breakfast and would tell us to eat at school, so we would always have to leave earlier to walk and get there on time. When we walked out the door, there was never a "Bye" or "See you guys after school," not even an "I love you." But I would hear my mother and Rocky talk sweetly to each other when he was in a good mood. In school, we never got questioned, and if we had black eyes or anything visible, we would miss school. That day in PE, I told the coach I was feeling a little better but was sore, so I sat out and didn't do anything.

As time passed and all the abuse was still going on, my mother just didn't ask us anything. It was as if she didn't care for us. What kind of mother doesn't protect her own children from monsters? We never had money. We didn't have great clothes. We didn't go anywhere but to a family member's home, and it was always so they could drink. We got to hang out with all our cousins and play on those nights. We sometimes even slept over. My mother didn't show any love. Maybe because she was never taught how to love. My mother could not comprehend a lot of things, and her education wasn't great. She couldn't help us with our homework since she dropped out in the sixth grade. My mother cussed a lot and yelled a lot as well. She was always stressed out and got angry so easily, especially the day we got evicted.

PART TWO

Adolescence

Is like having only enough light to see the step directly in front of you.

—Sarah Addison Allen

CHAPTER FOUR

The Move

O
ur landlord was a little old lady with ginger hair. She was always well-dressed and drove a fancy car. We only saw her once a month when rent was due and when she would check up on her other house in our lot that was used as her storage. We peeked a few times, and she had lots of antiques. It was so exciting to me, and I wanted to go in. So I did. I saw so many old Coca-Cola things and soda machines. I saw some unique glasses, so I took them. They had the words Betty Davis on the side. I obviously didn't know who that was at the time. That house was infested with roaches, spiders, opossums, and huge rats. My mother decided to call the city and make a report. The city came and checked on the house and we later saw that a red sticker was placed on the home. I overheard my mother saying that the little house needed to be demolished. Boy, that old lady showed up to the house very upset.

My mother told her that it was very dangerous due to how run-down it was, and the roof could collapse, plus all the rats. The landlord wasn't having it and told my mother we needed to move out right away. We started packing all our things, and I remember my uncles coming to help us out with a truck. We ended up moving not too far from the elementary school we went to, into a run-down apartment complex. But right before we left, my mother spray-painted "Bitch" on all the walls.

We moved into the Mohawk Apartments; they were yellow with brown trim around the windows. There were two strips of apartments, with caliche in the center of the complex. The apartment strips went from one side of Cheyenne Street to the other side of a different street, which was Mohawk Street. We had a corner efficiency apartment, and inside was a wall that separated the living room from the kitchen and bathroom and back door. The floor was basically a thin piece of wood that made noises as you walked around in the apartment. My mother had a bed in the living room by the front door where she and Rocky would sleep.

We went from a full-size bed that we shared to bunk beds that were right on the other side of the wall. We were basically in the kitchen area, and it sucked. As we got older, we couldn't stand sleeping with one another, but it was a normal dwelling for us. We had one TV in the living room, and if we watched any shows, we had to sit on the floor. It did not feel comfortable watching with Rocky lying on the bed behind us. At times, I had to sleep with one of my brothers on the twin bunk beds. First one on the bed was lucky. It was usually whoever had the bottom. Our bathroom was the worst. The toilet was old and too low. The sinks fixtures were old with lots of calcium buildup. The shower looked like a tall rectangular concrete box. It was dark inside with no lighting. There were always cobwebs with spiders or roaches inside. The hot water wouldn't last long, so we had to take a quick shower every day. We had to wait in between showers, and in the winter, it was cold as hell in that bathroom. I was terrified of that dang shower.

It was very uncomfortable for so many years, especially the days when Rocky would start hitting my brother. It happened with one of us in the bed. We couldn't say anything but just not move and wait to see if it was our turn. I would wake up so tired at times from staying up crying and hearing my brothers cry. It was sometimes hard to wake up to head to school. My mother would be right on the opposite of the wall and would do nothing. At times, he would come over to me and pick up the sheets at the end of my feet and use a flashlight to see under my shorts that I wore to bed with my brother right next to me. I hated him so much; he was disgusting. After a while, I started wearing my school clothes at night, which were always pants, so he would stop.

As my brothers and I got older, we started rebelling and hanging around the wrong crowds. My mother wouldn't ask us where we were or anything. There was no care in the world. We pretty much did what we wanted and came home when we wanted. Rocky and her wouldn't tell us anything. I think he started getting a little intimidated as we got older. We weren't really getting hit anymore. At times, I would go hang out with friends at the park and be up all night just to not come home and wait till the morning when he would leave for work. I would go home and sleep during the day.

One day, I was playing around with my friend Martha. Martha lived in the same apartment complex. I remember feeling something coming out of my private area. I was thirteen years old and had no clue what was going on. I kind of freaked out and told her I would be back. I ran to my apartment and went straight to the bathroom, and blood was running down my leg. My mother was in the kitchen, cooking, and I yelled out, "Mom!" I unlocked the door and told her I was bleeding. She walked in and locked the door behind us and told me I had started my period. I thought something was wrong with me, or maybe it was something Rocky did. My mother reached into the cabinet above the toilet, took out a pad, handed it to me, and told me to put it on and then walked back out into the kitchen.

My mouth dropped. *Is she not going to show me?* I knew how to put it on; we had seen some videos in class about it. I just thought a mother was supposed to have the talk with their daughters when this happened. I was thirteen years old, and no little girl at that age would want to deal with that. I went back to my friend's house and told her mother what happened, and she started to talk to me about the dos and don'ts while on my period. I needed all the advice I could get.

My mother didn't care what I was dealing with. It felt as if she were more concerned with what Rocky was doing. My mother was always making sure Rocky had his food ready and clothes washed, and of course, any chores that had to be done, I had to help. We didn't have a car, so when it was time to do the laundry, she made sure we always had a grocery basket from H-E-B to load up all the hampers in it so we could push it all the way to the Laundromat. I always complained because it was embarrassing to be seen by my friends, but she would force me. If not, I would get hit or my hair pulled. My mother didn't have much patience at all. I felt she was like this because she didn't have a mother. She was always mad unless she was drinking or high. I assumed it was the same thing for Rocky as well.

CHAPTER FIVE

Unprivileged Life

The first year I attended Martin Middle School, I was a good student. I wanted to be in everything. I loved the band, the pep squad, and the homemaking class. We didn't have much money, so I attended these classes for only a semester. Homemaking was very helpful; I was able to sew a lot of things I needed.

Students would talk about going to the Boys and Girls Club after school to play pool, basketball, or pretty much anything. It turned out to be my hangout. It was right next door to Martin Middle School. While talking to friends there, I overheard them say they had a DJ on Saturdays with awesome music. Dancing and singing were something I loved so much. I talked to Martha about going, and we started attending these dances. The music was hip hop rap that had some very explicit lyrics. The first time I attended, it was like the scene on the movie *Dirty Dancing*, when Baby walked into the staff party and saw everyone dancing in a very sexy, provocative way. In my time, if you danced that way, you were labeled as a slut or a pervert. I was shocked since I didn't dance this way.

I would attend these dances with Martha or my cousin Becky. All my other friends weren't allowed to be out past a certain time. We would have so much fun in that place, and we made so many friends. These events always ended at midnight, so we would either walk home or catch a ride with someone else. Violence around our city wasn't high then, so walking home at night was pretty normal.

Besides, it wasn't too far from home, and we were not the only ones who would walk home at those hours in our neighborhood.

I loved walking home at times so I could see my boy crush. I had a massive crush over this one guy who went to my school and the Boys and Girls Club. His name was Arturo, but they called him Tudy. He was a cute, bad boy who had short black hair that he would comb all the way back, sort of like a greaser. In our times, these guys were called cholos or even lowriders, although he didn't have a lowrider car. He lived a block away from the Boys and Girls Club. I would see him dance with his girlfriend at the time. Their dancing was literally like *Dirty Dancing*, and it made me wonder if he was sleeping with her already.

A week later, a friend told me that he was single. I was so excited and wanted to be his girlfriend so bad. How weird that this one girl came up to me and said hi and asked why I wasn't dancing. Turned out it was his sister Mara. I had Mara in a few classes, so I was assuming that was why she talked to me. I told her I didn't know how to dance in that way, so she told me just to follow what everyone was doing. Boy, was I nervous. Even worse, I didn't have a guy to dance with. I felt like I was the ugly duckling. Out of nowhere, Tudy came and grabbed my hand and said, "Come on, let's dance."

I started dancing apart from him, and then the next thing I know, he started getting closer and closer to me. I felt just like Baby when Patrick Swayze grabbed her and started dancing provocatively with her and she got all happy. I kept telling myself, *Please don't screw up. I hope I'm doing this right.* I could not stop laughing, and his ex-girlfriend kept staring at us dance. I knew she was mad and was probably going to want to start a fight, but I didn't care. Tudy finally asked me if I wanted a Coke or chips, and I said no. I couldn't think of eating or drinking anything at that moment. He then took my hand and had me follow him to a table to sit and talk. So he asked me for my name and said he saw me around at school but thought I looked too innocent. He started telling me that I was very pretty and asked if he could slide notes into my locker at times. Of course, I didn't hesitate to say yes. We talked so long that the lights came on, and the dance was over. I wanted to walk home with him so bad, but our ride was on the way to pick us up.

My friend Martha came running up to me and told me that his ex-girlfriend wanted to jump me—another term for coming up and telling me stuff to scare me. I was so afraid; I had never been in a fight before, especially over a guy. I saw a lot of people waiting outside for me, like if she was going to beat me up. I didn't want to walk out, so I told my best friend to let me know when her brother was coming for us.

Laura ended up walking back in and asked me why was I riding her boyfriend. The term *riding* meant "grinding" as they call it nowadays.

"He told me you guys weren't together anymore," I said.

"So?" she said.

I was not going to fight this girl, especially when I learned earlier that day that she was still in elementary school. Our ride showed up, and we just walked out. I was scared as hell.

That Monday, I went back to school and was told that she was going to be outside to beat me up. She attended Crockett Elementary School, which was right next door to Martin, so she could easily come to my school. That day, I received a letter from Tudy in my locker. Oh, the sweet words he wrote. I had a smile the whole day, but behind all that, I was still scared of fighting. I wrote back to Tudy and slipped it in his locker. I wrote to him and told him how I had always had a crush on him. I was afraid of what he was going to think of me. *Was I too straight forward with telling him how I felt?* I had more important things to think about, like getting my butt kicked after school. Then came three o'clock, and I walked outside the front door of the school and didn't see anything out of the ordinary. I walked home with my friends and just forgot about it.

The next day was pretty much the same, except this time, he asked me to meet him after school so he could walk me home. I was so worried about what to do if he tried to kiss me. I had never kissed a boy before. *What if he wanted to make out?* I could not concentrate at all that day. Three o'clock came, and I walked to the back of the school. And there he was, smiling. He reached out for my hand, and we started walking around the field of the school. Then he asked me if I wanted to be his girlfriend. I was so shy and said yes. I was expecting a kiss, but he walked me home and said he would see me at school the following day. He was waiting for me at my locker the next morning. I was so happy. He asked if he could walk me to my classes, and of course, I wasn't about to say no.

Things were great between us. I got close to his sisters and brothers, and he had me go over to meet his parents. It was fast and crazy. One thing I didn't mention was that all the girls were crazy for Tudy, and he was also in a gang, but I didn't care. I started drinking and smoking marijuana with him. I started skipping classes and taking off with him and friends to hang out at parks. We would get into fights with other gangs. The day of the gang initiation, I was punched and kicked by a bunch of girls and had to fight back to prove my worth to them.

I just didn't care. My mother didn't stick up for me, but they did. I started always hanging around Tudy and his sisters and fighting a lot and skipping classes. On the weekends, we would walk to ballrooms to attend quinceañeras of our friends. One tragic night, we decided to go to a quinceañera at the Galvan Ballroom. We always had to have a plan in case a fight broke out. There were lots of people who didn't care too much for Tudy. I always would say it was the jealousy.

A bunch of us were all there having a good time, and he decided to go outside for a smoke break. Tudy was talking to his best friend, Jerry, who was his ex-girlfriend's brother. Jerry was so cool and just loved to laugh and joke around. I was so high and buzzed. I don't remember who I was talking to, and all you could hear around that area were the vehicles on the highway. Outside the ballroom was an underpass and the road called Agnes. Traffic was always heavy around there. I remember hearing shots that sounded kind of like fireworks, and when I turned to look at Tudy and Jerry, they were both on the ground. I stood there in shock while everyone ran. I couldn't move for a bit, and next thing I know, I was screaming. I dropped to my knees and felt like I had just gotten punched in the chest so hard, and I couldn't breathe. I saw black, and I remember seeing the ambulance there and taking them. I heard someone say Tudy was dead on the ground and Jerry was on the way to the hospital. My boyfriend was gone! I don't remember how I got home, but I drank and cried so much that night I passed out.

CHAPTER SIX

Forward Frustrations

It was 1989, my first year as a freshman. I was excited especially because a few of my good friends were all going to be there. I heard so many rumors about Roy Miller High School. The school had a bad reputation because of its location, the North Side.

I grew up on the West Side, which also had a bad reputation, so it didn't bother my friends or me. After what happened to Tudy, this change kept me away from the gang. Most of the guys in the gang went to Moody High School, but because of my district area, I had to attend Miller. It was confusing. Moody High School was way closer than Miller. Well, guess what, Eva Longoria was a student there as well. We had a few friends in common but never talked. It was exciting to know she became such a huge celebrity.

The school was huge, three floors high, and still had portables outside for other classes. And don't get me started on our stadium. This stadium was one of the biggest in Corpus Christi, and our football team was awesome. I went to so many games and after-school dances, and pep rallies with my friends. At times, I didn't always go home at night because my stepfather was home. I didn't trust him and didn't want to be bothered by him at night looking under my sheets and trying to touch me. Other than that, my best friends and I would walk home or ride the school bus after school and always ended up at my place. Those were the days that the five of us got so close and had so much fun.

April would always cook *fideo*, which is also known as vermicelli, while Erika, Kathy, Letty, and I would sing to boys on the phone and dance to our favorite boy band, like New Kids on the Block. I felt as if I had two lives. By day, I was a good, fun teenager, and by night, I was hanging around the wrong crowd and still smoking and drinking. It eventually got to the point where I would miss school at times just to go home to sleep when Rocky wasn't there. My mother, of course, wouldn't say anything or even ask what I was up to. I hated my mother and didn't really talk much to her.

A mother should protect her children from anyone who tries to do them harm, especially from another man. I knew she was going through her bad relationship with Rocky, him hitting her and them always drinking and getting drunk. The best thing I felt I could do was leave home and just hang out with my friends. I had a friend named Frank, and we talked a lot in school and sometimes on the phone if I was home. I would tell him about my boy crush Mario and how I felt. I wanted to talk to him so bad.

One day, on the school bus, one of my friends told Mario I liked him. I was so embarrassed. That school bus would drop him off first down his block. My friends and I were usually last. I was so in love with this jock; it was nothing like Tudy. Mario was popular in school. We ended up finally talking and would sit together on the bus, talk, and laugh. He was always smiling and in a good mood. Mario asked me for my number one day, and I gave it to him. That meant I definitely had to be home to get his calls. It was the eighties, and there was no such thing as cell phones. If somebody said they would call you at seven, well, you pretty much had to sit near the phone waiting.

I actually sacrificed staying at home just to talk to him. Rocky would tell us we couldn't be on the phone late and we couldn't even watch TV where we slept. I would put up with everything just to hear what Mario had to say. We would talk about things we went through with our families. I just never told him of Rocky. He would play songs and sing to me. He would tell me a few of his secrets he didn't want the boys to know. He was a sweet guy and had me in a great mood, so I kept a journal and started writing away. Thanks to him, I kept writing after all these years.

I would sit outside and write down all my thoughts and feelings about us and how he treated me. Mario called me one night and said he had his father's van and asked if I wanted to go for a ride. Of course, I said yes. I didn't really wear makeup, and I wasn't the type to wear skirts or dresses and get all dolled up. So jeans and a T-shirt it was. Mario showed up and drove me around. I was so nervous; my hands were so clammy when he held them. We ended our night at a park he enjoyed. We took a walk and talked for a bit. He couldn't be out too late. On the way home, he told me he really liked me and that he hoped to see me in school the next day.

I walked into the apartment and started writing away about him in my journal. I was so happy at that moment. Rocky walked up to me with his fist right under my nose and slapped my journal out of my hands. He yelled out, "Don't be coming in late or else!" I didn't respond, so he shoved his fist even harder up my nose. I pulled away, and he walked back to the living room / bedroom. I just stopped writing and lay in bed, expecting him to bother me that night, but nothing happened.

The next day, Mario and I didn't talk much. He had a pep rally to attend and a football game. I went home on the school bus that day. I got home, and suddenly, Rocky started yelling at me. I was going nuts and felt a little sad that I hadn't talked to Mario the whole day, so it didn't bother me at all what Rocky was even saying.

"I read what you wrote in your journal, and you like that he kissed you?"

I didn't say anything to him, but I did try to take my journal, and he started tearing it up. I was so mad and filled with anger. I couldn't believe he was reading and looking through my personal things. It was as if he were jealous and were mad that I had someone. He slapped me in the face, and I ran out of the house and stayed at a friend's house for two days. I talked to Mario over the phone and let him know what was going on at home. He told me he would pick me up at my friend's house after football practice and take me home. He told me I needed to go home and talk things out with my stepfather. Stepfather? This monster didn't deserve to be called stepfather. Mario didn't know everything Rocky had been doing to me and my brothers. All he knew was that I got in trouble for my journal. He picked me up and took me to his house to talk.

That night, one thing led to another, and I slept with him for the first time. He thought I was a virgin, but with everything Rocky did to me, I wasn't. I was so confused that I even asked myself if I was a virgin because he was the first boy I had ever slept with. How could that be though with everything Rocky did to me? So I just agreed with Mario and told him I was. He told me he felt bad because he wasn't a virgin. Things were a little awkward after that. I told him to take me home. I walked in, and everyone was asleep. I took the phone to the bathroom with me in case he called me. As soon as he got home, he called and asked if I talked to Rocky. I told him I needed to shower and everyone was asleep. He suddenly blurted out that I needed to tell my mother what we did because the condom he wore busted. I freaked out, so I hung up and turned the ringer off.

I got to school the next morning, and he was waiting for me down the hallway by my locker. "I will tell my mother tonight," I said. Mario insisted that he was gonna call me after school and that he wanted to be on the phone when I did tell my mother. "What the hell! How is this gonna make me feel? Do you know how loud my mother yells?" I said. He wasn't having it. I saw my friend Frank standing outside a class we had together. Frank was someone who I would sometimes confide in. I told Frank what happened and that I needed some advice. He got upset and walked into the classroom.

"That was a big mistake." he said. "Why with him? Do you know what kind of guy he is?"

I just walked off to class.

Mario called me that evening and made me tell my mother. My mother was cooking in the kitchen, and I was in the bathroom, talking to him. I opened the door and asked her to come into the bathroom so I could tell her something.

She yelled out, "What do you want?"

At this point, I was afraid, and I pictured all that grease in the pan of fried chicken being thrown at me. "Mario told me to tell you we had sex." I said it so fast and dropped the phone. My mother yelled at me and said she was going to have me take a pregnancy test in a month.

Well, two weeks went by, and the next thing I know, Mario and I started arguing. He became distant, and not so long after that, we just quit talking. When the time came to check if I was pregnant, my period came. I didn't talk to him, and he didn't care to ask either. I still attended school and a few dances here and there, but I mainly started hanging out with a different crowd in the North Side.

Frank decided to ask me out and told me he liked me and asked if I would give him a chance. I did, and we were together for a year before his true colors started to show. He started being very possessive, controlling, and was a very jealous person. At school one day, he started yelling in my face. I walked away and started going into a hallway. He grabbed me and pinned me up against the wall. All the football players would stand up against the wall until the bell would ring for first period. As soon as they saw what he was doing, they all rushed up to him and pulled him off me.

Principal Powers came running down the hallway to stop everything and made everyone get to class. I ended up skipping the rest of the day after first period just so I wouldn't have to see Frank. I hung out at a friend's place and ended up going home the next day. I didn't want to go to school, so I just stayed home. Rocky went to work, so I thought I would be okay. I heard someone knocking at my door very hard; it was Frank! I didn't answer, so it made him more upset. He drove off so fast all I heard were the tires burning rubber. He peeled out his car right in front of our apartment. I freaked out and hoped he wouldn't come back later when everyone was home. My mom came home from work and started cooking dinner. I heard a knock at the door again, and my heart dropped. It was him. I went outside because I didn't want my mom and Rocky to start anything with Frank. Frank started apologizing and told me it would never happen again. I believed him, and we were fine after that for a while.

PART THREE

The Second Battle

Choose your battles wisely. After all, life isn't measured by how many times you stood up to fight. It's not winning battles that makes you happy, but it's how many times you turned away and chose to look into a better direction. Life is too short to spend it on warring. Fight only the most, most, most important ones, let the rest go.

—C. JoyBell C.

CHAPTER SEVEN

A Child Having a Child

My mother woke me up one morning and literally had a cup in front of my face and told me I needed to pee inside it. I asked her what for. She said she needed to turn it in to a clinic to see if I was pregnant. I asked her why, and she said she knew I hadn't had my period in a while since we all shared the same bathroom.

Talk about mothers know everything, so why didn't she do anything about Rocky? I didn't know what the hell I was doing, but I managed to pee in the cup. Tests would be in on the following day, so all we could do was wait. The next day, we went to the clinic, and the results came back positive. My mother was upset but wasn't loud as usual. I was in shock. *Is she about to hit me?* The doctor told her she was surprised to see that she wasn't yelling at me.

"The job is done, and there is nothing I can do about it now," said my mother. There was silence on the way home.

"Well?" said Rocky. She nodded. Of course, he had something to say, but it wasn't anything I wasn't used to already. All I could think about was, I didn't want my baby around him.

I left and took off to my friend's house and told her everything. I hadn't told Frank yet because I knew he was going to be worried about his parents and what they would say. Frank's parents were good people. His dad was in the military, and his mother was a housekeeper.

The following day, Frank picked me up for school, and I was trying to figure out how to tell him. In a low voice, I told him we were having a baby. He was happy, but I could see that he was scared as well. In my mind, I was freaking out and questioning why the hell he was happy. I didn't want a child with him; we still had issues with his anger and how selfish he was. I left it at that, and the next thing I know, everyone in school found out. I got called into the office by the principal. I didn't know what was going on. The principal told me no one was allowed to attend public school pregnant. Apparently, it brought a lot of embarrassment and distractions to the schools.

I had to transfer to a school named TAMS (Teenage Mother School). I was actually excited that we could eat as much as we wanted during lunch or in class. I was also told I could leave when I wanted if I didn't feel good. That was even better since the school was down the street from the apartment. They took into consideration that being pregnant came with complications at times. I felt great and didn't go through any morning sickness.

Frank went through it all. He told his parents, and they were very upset. They were expecting a lot from him, and I understood that. He got a job and was helping me and would stay with me at times at the apartment. Nobody cared for him there. My brothers had to sleep together now because my belly was getting bigger, so that made it worse. Frank and I barely fit in the bed, but I didn't care. I was comfortable with the fact that Rocky wouldn't be bothering me at night anymore.

After a while, I felt like the pressure was more and more stressful, and Frank wasn't a very nice person at times. I wasn't allowed to wear makeup or even dress up. He was a very jealous person. He still had the mentality of a single person, and all his money went to his car. Of course, I had to get government assistance, so he would have more money in his pocket to buy the parts for his car, radio, etc. I was starting to despise him. All I could think was that my son needed to have a father. I couldn't leave him and do it alone. My due date was getting closer, and everything started getting uncomfortable for me. It was harder to walk home from school on the days he was working.

On June 28, 1991, morning came, and I started having contractions, so we rushed to the ER. Everything was pretty fast; it wasn't too long before I had to start pushing. My mother and Frank were in the delivery room. I pushed a few times, and my son, Frankie, was out quick, eight pounds and three ounces. My mother was in shock and asked Frank to go check the weight again. I didn't get too big, so no one thought the baby would be huge. It was accurate. I could barely walk, and I felt so tired. The doctor told me I would be in the hospital for two days.

The following day, Frank went home to bring more clothes and necessities. He showed up back with my cousin Mary, whom I was close to at one time and who also lived at the apartments. She was a lot older than us. Don't you know, this jerk had the nerve to tell me he was going to the movies with her! There I was still in the hospital bed, hurting and tired, and that was all he could think about instead of his son. I was furious; I didn't want to see him. *What the hell is wrong with this guy? Is he cheating on me with my own cousin?* I didn't want to even think about it.

On the day of my release, it was time to take my son, whom I named Frankie, home. Frank wasn't at the hospital at the time; he knew I was upset. I had to call him to take us home, and he showed up late, of course.

At the apartment, my mother said I could start sleeping in the living room since we had a crib now. Frank's mother was eager to see the baby, and when she showed up, all I got was that crazy look because of the way we lived. We didn't have much; we were all crammed up in that efficiency apartment, but at least it was always very clean. Frank told me later that day that his mom wanted us to move into their house because we needed a bigger space, and they had a big house with an apartment in the back. I agreed, and we moved so we could have our own room. The whole house had air-conditioning—that was a luxury for someone like me—and our room was big. Frank continued working and coming home late while I was there taking care of the baby. His mother helped, but she wanted it her way at all times.

I complained a lot to him, so he talked to his parents to see if we could move to the apartment they had in the back of the house. His parents said yes as long as we paid the rent, and water and light were included. That was our little home. It was a little exciting at first up until I noticed he was always showing up smelling like other women, coming home too late, with all these lies he fed me. Every time I would argue back, I would get hit, or he would pin me down on the bed while I cried and pretty much rape me when I would tell him to stop. I wasn't afraid of him, of all the things Rocky had done to me. The physical pain was nothing.

If I yelled, all he would do was cover my mouth so his parents wouldn't hear. Their bedroom was at the back of the house, which was close to our front door. When he was done, he would just act like nothing happened. I finally told his mother the things he did to me, and she asked me what I did to provoke him. Things got pretty bad with us, and he started going out on his own and leaving me home. I was just a piece of meat that was there for him. He blew his money on himself and rent. He couldn't miss rent, of course, and have his mom upset. My feelings didn't matter. I decided to move back to my mother's.

He went looking for me and banged on the door and tried to hit me. His temper was bad. "You will come back," he said, and I always did. Every time I looked at my son, all I could think about was how good he was to him. I didn't want another man in my life who was going to abuse my son the way it happened to my brothers and myself.

I was back and forth to my mother's, until the day came when I had had enough and decided I needed to do something with myself for my son's sake. At my mother's apartment, we wouldn't always lock the door. He drove up one day and walked right in without knocking and went straight up to me and hit me in the ribs while I was holding Frankie. I couldn't breathe, and I was gasping for air. "I hate you," he said and walked out and took off in his car. We didn't see him for a few months, and one day, he decided to show up, saying he wanted to see Frankie. My son looked at him like he was a stranger. I told him to take me to court because I wasn't going to let my son go with him.

The only reason he was there was because his dad wanted to see him before he got deployed. Wow! Didn't seem to me like he was interested in his son. We attended court, and he had to start paying child support now. He also received his visitation rights, which gave him the right to pick up Frankie every other weekend. He would never show up until his father had to leave again. This time, he showed up with police officers. I had no choice but to let him take him. He had the paperwork, so it was out of my hands. My son cried and screamed; a stranger was taking him. I cried with so much worry—worried if they knew how to take care of him. *Is he going to be able to sleep without me?* I couldn't take it; I had so much hate toward Frank.

I couldn't be at home without my son; I felt like I was going crazy. That Sunday, I was home waiting for Frankie to get dropped off. When he showed up, he looked fine and happy. That was a relief for me. After that, my son didn't see his father again until his new girlfriend asked if she could pick him up for Frank. His girlfriend, Lisa, and I talked for a while. She was a very understanding person with a good head on her shoulders. Her intentions were good. She explained to me that his dad was in prison and was given an eight-year sentence. I didn't ask why; I just knew things were going to be different from now on. She would show up every other weekend and buy him clothes or whatever my son needed. Frankie did get attached to her as well. I was at ease and moved on with my life. Things were good.

CHAPTER EIGHT

Adulting

One afternoon, I decided to take my son to the Greenwood pool. I stopped at a corner neighborhood store, QC Meat Market. Back then, I believe it had a different name, but everyone in the neighborhood went there to get their snacks, deli meat, or just hang out outside. Everyone knew one another around there.

That day, I noticed a guy rushing out of there while I was walking in. I did a double take and noticed it was Alex. I stopped and looked for the car but noticed he got into a small blue pickup. That was weird. I never thought he would get rid of that awesome car. Alex was Melissa's brother-in-law, my mother's good friend. He also lived at the apartment complex and drove this very loud gold Trans-Am with an eagle on the hood of the car. I was in love with that car and was crazy about just how fast that car went.

There were a few times, while in middle school, that he gave Martha and me a ride to school especially if the weather was too bad. He was a lot older and loved loud music. There was no use in talking to each other if we were in his car, and I thought that was funny. Girls were crazy about him in school; they would literally throw themselves at him.

Well, after spending the day at the pool, I noticed a little blue pickup across the street from our apartment that looked exactly like the one I saw Alex in at the meat market. I thought our friends Adam and Lisa lived in that house. Did they move out? Was Alex related to them too? I wasn't too curious, so I just forgot about it for a while and didn't pay any attention. I walked or went on the bus everywhere, unless I had to go to work, then I would call a cab. I was talking to my friend on the phone, and she told me to hang out with her at the Greenwood pool. As I walked down the street, I saw Alex, but in a different car—a car that I usually see in the driveway at the house across the street. There was another girl in the car, so I figured maybe he got married or something. I got to the pool, and on the way back, I saw him again. I thought it was weird that I kept running into him.

As I got home, I saw him walk out and start washing his truck. I wanted to call out his name but thought it would be rude, especially if he was married, so I kept walking. I decided to walk to the meat market later that evening while my mother watched Frankie. I needed some deli meat to take to work for lunch. I started walking, and then I heard a honk. It was him slowing down on the side of the sidewalk. He rolled down the window, and I freaked out! It was *not* Alex! This guy was a total stranger but was like his twin! I was in shock on how identical they looked.

"You want a ride?" he asked.

"No," I replied.

"I am just going down the street."

"Do you usually pick up girls this way?"

His response was, "No!" He was mad.

I guess this guy wasn't used to rejection. I got to the store and went to the deli in the back of the store. As I walked up to the front, I saw him walking in and grabbing a soda. He walked toward the back of the store where I was standing and said, "Are you following me?"

I laughed and walked up to the front and put my stuff down on the counter. He told the cashier he was also paying for my things. That caught me off guard, and it actually felt good. He asked If I wanted to go back home with him since I lived right across the street, but I still said no. He smacked his lips and walked out. I thought it was so funny how hard he was trying, but it was cute at the same time. I walked back home and saw him sitting outside on his porch, staring.

"Hey, you!" he yelled out.

"What's up?" I yelled out.

"Come over here," he said.

I told him to wait, and I never showed up. I fell asleep so hard and was so tired, especially with all the sun and walking. The following day, I took Frankie outside to play with his toys. I couldn't stand being inside when Rocky was there. It was starting to feel a little better when my mother was there because she was starting to stand up for herself and us. Rocky wasn't really hitting anyone anymore. My brothers were older and meaner and now stood up for themselves. Rocky was more about playing with Frankie and doing things for him, but that still didn't change all the anger I had toward him. It was crazy how a child can change a lot in a home. Although he was still doing his drugs, he wasn't as bad as he was when we were a lot younger.

I was outside, and I saw my neighbor whom I called Alex come out and sit on his steps, and he waved. I waved back, and I went about my business and played with my son. My mother got home from work, and usually, when she was home, she would take Frankie and play with him or take him to the store to buy him something. I walked to a friend's house, and there came the neighbor and asked me again if I wanted a ride. This time, I said yes. I figured since it was literally half a block away, why not, and I got in the car. I asked about his truck, and he said he was having issues.

He asked me for my name, and at that time, everyone called me Angela. I never understood why—on my birth certificate, it said Angelica—but it was what my family always called me. He told me his name was Max. I told him the whole deal about Alex, and he laughed. We got to my friend's house, and he asked me if he could take me to dinner that Friday. I hadn't gone out on a date with anyone besides Mario and Frank.

We went to dinner that Friday night. The conversation was good. He was a charmer, and I found myself wondering if he was a cheater. After dinner, we took a walk at the beach and joked around. I started feeling uncomfortable as he was being too touchy and was trying to hold my hand and hug me. I had to tell him to stop. I didn't know much about this guy, so why would he think it was okay to do all those things right away? *Does this guy think I was easy?* He took me home and gave me a kiss on the cheek. I felt okay, but not excited, didn't have any of the butterflies going on.

I usually stayed up late and would sit outside with the neighbors, talking. This time, I went outside to talk on the phone. The phone cord was so long I could take that thing anywhere. I called my best friend Erika to tell her how the date went. I looked up and noticed he was leaving again. I told Erika, and she started putting things in my head and laughing, telling me he probably went to go pick up another girl. I thought it was funny, but I caught myself taking a look at my watch—it was 10:00 p.m. What she said stayed in the back of my head. I went inside and started watching TV. I looked at my watch again after a while, and it was 1:00 a.m., and I still didn't see the truck in his driveway. The next morning, I looked out the window and saw his truck there.

I didn't think much the following day. I got my son, and I dressed up to go to the mall. We always went on the bus, and Frankie loved it. We got to the mall and walked around, and I decided I wanted to get him an outfit. We had a Mervyn's store at the time, and there were always cute kid clothes there. I walked in, and I saw Max there with another girl and with a baby on a stroller. I was in shock because he didn't tell me he had a baby or a girlfriend or a wife. Talk about busted. He looked at me and turned away quickly. The first thought that came to mind was my friend on the phone last night. I kept walking, and since they were in the kid's section, I went to the women's section and decided to just go down the escalator to the rest of the mall. I took my son to eat and figured I would just wait it out for a bit until I went back. Eventually, I went and got my son his outfit and then got on the bus to head home. On the way home, I had my mind on all these questions I felt I needed to ask him. He must had been looking for a one-night stand. Was he just a player? What was wrong with this guy?

I got home and bathed my son. I called Erika and told her to pick me up so we could go hangout with some friends. My mother never liked my son to be with me because of the type of people I would hang out with. So she would take care of Frankie whenever I wanted to go out. Erika picked me up, and that night, we got drunk. My friend decided to leave the car at the party, and we walked home. I got home, and my mother was still up and told me Max had called a couple of times. I got so angry and started to dial his number, but then I stopped and told myself not to be a kiss ass. I needed to just kill him with kindness and ignore him.

Morning came, and I was up eating breakfast with my son. I had work at 5:00 p.m., so I took my son outside to play with him before my cab got there. I saw Max pull out of his driveway, and in my mind, I was hoping he wouldn't come down my way. But he did! He pulled up to the curb and called me to the car. He told me he'd been calling me. I gave him a simple "Oh." He started explaining to me that the girl I saw him with was his baby mama and that she needed to buy clothes for his son.

"I am not your girlfriend. I will talk to you later. I am busy with my son." He asked if we could talk later, and I said, "Yes, after work."

Later that night, I got home, and I saw that he was outside sitting on his steps. He waved at me to go over. I walked up, and he grabbed my hand and asked if I was mad.

I pulled away and said, "No."

He was trying to explain why he had to pick her up all the time. "That's the only way I could see my son," he said.

"I wasn't born yesterday, Max," I replied. I knew how the whole visitation thing worked. I told him, "Look, I'm not your girlfriend, and I don't know what you want from me."

"I want to get to know you and see where it goes," he said.

I didn't hold my breath, but it seemed as if the more of an ass-hole I was, the more he would call. We went on a few dates, and he never tried anything. But I did see some red flags, so I tried to keep my walls up. One Thursday afternoon, he walked over and asked me if I could go with him over the weekend. He offered to pay my mother to babysit. That was a big *wow* for me. Didn't think any man would do that just to spend time with me.

He took me to his hometown, George West, Texas. He had family there, and they were very nice people. He rented a room, and we went to a festival they had there. He introduced me to a lot of his friends. Later that night, we hung out with his buddies and their wives and drank for a bit. When we got to the room, I just threw myself on the bed and passed out. The next morning, I looked over and saw that he was lying on the floor, and I tapped him with my foot. He woke up laughing, and I asked why he was on the floor. He said he was being a gentleman.

"I like gentlemen," I said.

"Good, because you will always have that with me," he said.

This guy is good! I told myself.

I jumped in the shower, and we started to get ready so we could have breakfast at his uncle's house. I got to meet more family. They told us to stick around for some BBQ for dinner. I had a great time with them; they were a very well-mannered and loving family. We went back to the room and called it a night. That Sunday, we went to church with his family, had lunch, and said our prayers, and then we headed straight home. He dropped me off, and this time, he reached over for a kiss. I had a big smile on my face.

He wanted to get to know my son and took us both out too. *Could he be the one?* Things went good for a bit. We both worked and went out to dinners and took Frankie with us at times and took him to the park and movies. Until one day, I saw Anna, his baby mama, walking out of his house and yelling. I saw police officers pulling up and knew something was wrong. She had his son in her arms, and I saw Max crying. I let things calm down and waited for him to call me. He called me after a few days and said that he was having a lot of issues and that they were going to interfere with our relationship. His number 1 priority was his son, and I totally understood that.

We didn't talk for about two weeks, and I didn't see him. I knew his mother, and she would see me and wave from across the street or if she passed by my apartment from time to time. One day, I got a phone call while I was at home, and it was him. He told me he missed me and couldn't stop thinking about me. As naive as I was, I believed him. At eighteen years old, I was still pretty naive. I asked him how things were going, and he told me not too good. She wouldn't let him see his son much unless she was around was what he said. I had a gut feeling he was lying, but at that age, we tend to not follow our intuitions, especially when you think you're in love.

He asked me out again and asked me to go away with him again to George West. We left on a Saturday morning and met up with his friends and stayed at their home. He showed me a home that was under construction and told me it was his and that if I was lucky, I could be moving in with him.

I thought, *Wow! This guy has his stuff together. This is what I need.* He had a great job in law enforcement, but I just wasn't sure if we were going in the same direction.

We left home the following day, and he told me he was going to start working nights. I wasn't going to see much of him because he would sleep during the day, but we could talk over the phone. I went out one night with some friends, and that same night, he called me and said he needed to talk to me in the morning. Morning came, and he looked upset and asked me if I thought all this was a game.

"What are you talking about?" I said.

He said to me, "I know you went out last night."

"So?" I replied. Confused, I asked, "Are we a couple? Is this serious?" I freaked out, and then I got upset. I was about to walk away, and he grabbed my arm and told me he was sorry for not telling me how he felt. He gave me a necklace, and that was his way of asking me to be his girl. *These Southern men have a way of doing things, huh?*

Things were good for a few months, until I started noticing his son's things in his room while I was at work. There were diapers in the trash and toys around his room. It doesn't take a genius to see when things look different in a small room. My guess was Anna was going over. All this was taking place while I was at work during the day. So I confronted him about it, and he told me his mother was able to go pick him up from now on. Then the drama came after that. I overheard a conversation between him and his mother. I couldn't make out what they were arguing about, but it had to do with Anna. I asked him what was going on, and he told me in order to see his son, it had to be supervised visits with her around. He said to me that she would be okay if I was there.

Day 1 was okay. Day 2, I went to go get my son, and I didn't think anything about them being there because his mother, stepfather, and sister were there as well. Until I came back that day and she was gone. I went into the room, and I saw a condom in the trash. I walked right out of that house and went straight home. He came knocking, and I told everyone to not answer. He then called the phone, but there was no answer.

The following day, I saw him crossing the street, and I walked outside. He kept saying sorry over and over again. He had the nerve to tell me that she seduced him. I yelled at the top of my lungs, "Who in the hell doesn't know when they're doing something wrong?" I don't get when people say shit like "Oh, in the heat of the moment. Sure, buddy!" "Just leave me alone!" I said.

He said he wasn't going to. He kept bugging and bugging every day. Eventually, I forgave him, and we got back together. She wouldn't let him see his son as long as he was with me. Max didn't want to follow the court agreement and called officers to go over. He didn't want to put his son through that or for everyone to start talking about his personal life at work. Things got bad between her and me, and so many problems came about even with her sisters. He and his mother ended up moving a few blocks down. He didn't see his son for a bit, and he wanted me over there every day. But we both had work, so why would I be over there all the time?

I would go on my days off and hang out when he was there, until my son and I moved in. Things were okay for a bit, but then I started having issues with his mother. She wanted his son over, so she did what it took to have him over, and that meant having his baby mama too. She would do these things without telling Max or myself. I had no say so because it was her house. I would get home from work, and it sucked to see his baby mama there in the house. All kinds of things ran through my head. *Are they up to something? Are they looking through my things?* I started to go over to my mother's apartment on my days off just so I wouldn't feel uncomfortable. Max would pick us up after work and take us back with him. I hated it.

Well, one day, I realized my menstrual cycle was late. I went to the clinic, and I was told I was pregnant. I told him that day, and he was upset and said he couldn't have another child. It wasn't the answer I wanted to hear. He gave me money and told me to go get an abortion. *I freaked out and cried!* I got all my clothes and told him to drop me off at my mom's apartment.

I would talk to his sister from time to time; she slipped and let the cat out of the bag. His baby mama was pregnant too! He was cheating on me with Anna the whole time. I felt so stupid for being naive. I was so angry. I took that money and bought a onesie and bootees for a newborn and put it in a gift bag and gave it to him. I told him, "Here is your gift, and I am not getting an abortion." He told me he had decided to get back with her. That just made me feel worse and tore me up inside. I cried to his sister Isabel, and she told me she would be there for me.

A week later, she invited my son and me to the carnival. We went, and she introduced me to a friend of hers, Roy. He was cute and all, but come on, I was pregnant. He wanted to take me out, but I told him I couldn't because I was pregnant.

"If you're pregnant, you got to eat," he said. He said he didn't care and that my baby daddy was a douchebag. Max's sister had told him everything. I told him I didn't need him feeling sorry for me. He didn't care. "You are a beautiful and strong woman," he said.

Roy and I dated. Max never bothered to check up on me. He didn't care. He had an apartment with Anna and his son. I assumed things were great for him. So I did what I had to and moved on with Roy.

He was such a hard worker and a great guy, but I didn't love him. Roy didn't care; he just wanted to be with me and take care of me and my son and the baby. He told me he was going to help me get my license and get back to finishing school, and I did. He even went out and got an apartment for us. Things were good!

On December 28, 1994, when my daughter, Victoria, was born, Roy was the only one there in the delivery room. I was hoping I would see my daughter's father there, but nothing. If a man wants to be there for his child, he will find a way and try very hard.

I was released and stayed home until Victoria's first doctor's appointment. I was driving down Morgan Avenue, and I saw Max's mother. She passed me up, and I looked out my rearview mirror and saw that she was making a U-turn. *Oh brother, here we go with the drama queen.* Everyone knew pretty much what I drove. I had a royal-blue pickup with shiny rims and what they call ghost patterns that Roy had bought me. It was a show truck we would use for car shows. She followed me all the way to the store where I pulled over to see what she wanted. She said all she wanted was to see her grand-daughter. She knew I had Victoria already. That woman was a good investigator I might say. She asked if I could take her to her house to see her, and I told her I had to talk to Roy.

"Why? He isn't the father," she asked.

"He was there through the whole thing, and your son wasn't. So just because he knocked me up doesn't give him a say so, especially when he wanted me to have an abortion," I replied. She told me to think it over. I went home and talked to Roy about it, and he said he didn't have a problem with it.

"Victoria is part of their family, and she needs to know them," he said. I told him she promised Max wouldn't be there. Roy reassured me things would be okay.

The following day, I showed up to her house, and they were all excited to see Victoria. Everyone was taking pictures and holding her. Behold, the front door opened, and Max walked in, carrier in hand with his new baby and son.

"I didn't know he was coming," she said.

I was so upset. She must have planned this. I should have known after her evil ways.

Max grabbed Victoria, stared at her, and said, "Finally, a daughter."

I started putting her things in the truck and told them it was time to go. Max asked if we could talk regarding Victoria. I told him no. Things started getting worse after that. He found out where I lived and would come knocking as soon as Roy would leave for work. He must have ran my plates or something. I never answered the door. One day, while I was walking out and getting into the truck, Max pulled up. I tried to rush to get Frankie and Victoria in so we could leave. He said all he wanted was to talk to me about Victoria. I told him to talk quick before I change my mind and to get it over with.

It went from talking about her for, like, ten minutes to talking about me. He was quite the charmer, and I still loved him. He started telling me how miserable he was with Anna and how he always imagined how things would be between us as a family. He promised me things would be different and that he would leave her. I ended up talking to Roy and moved out. He knew that day was coming; he knew I didn't love him. Max gave up his apartment, and we moved into his mother's house. Everyone asked why I would leave from having it all to living with my mother-in-law.

Love can be very blind and make you do stupid things. I was still young. Of course, things were good for a while, but then it started again. Baby mama started going over with his sons because he couldn't pick them up. It was always Max's mother who started all the drama. I was attending Vogue College, so I would leave to class or go to my mother's just so I wouldn't see them.

One night, it was so cold and rainy outside. Victoria was about a year old, barely starting to walk. Max picked me up from my mother's, and we went home. As soon as we walked in, we saw Anna there with his sons and his mother. Nobody said hi, and his mother started yelling at us, asking if we thought her house was a fucking hotel. We were so confused as to what was going on. She told us to get our stuff and leave. I couldn't believe it after all the bullshit I heard about wanting her granddaughter around blah, blah, blah. We had no money and nowhere to go. We ended up staying at his cousin's house, and he said it was okay until we got back on our feet.

That same day, I was told my father had passed away from meningitis and alcoholism. We talked at times, but not as close as we once were. As far as I knew, he had a girlfriend who was pregnant with twins, and till this day, I have yet to meet them. I was told she gave them up to a family member. I have tried to look for them but haven't succeeded.

My mind was going crazy. I was so stressed out and hurt. I felt like just running away to a place where everything could be better. Jesus put this in my life, so I had to face it all and deal with it. I couldn't quit; I had children who needed me. It wasn't long before we got married, and we moved out and got our own apartment. We asked his mother for our furniture that we had in her storage so we could take them to our new apartment. She told Max she had a garage sale and sold it all because she needed money. She just put so much hate inside me. We moved out of his cousin's house and had to start buying things slowly. Things were okay for a bit, but then he started cheating on me again. I always found numbers, stains of women's lipstick on his clothing, marks on his chest, and suspicious phone calls. Max even went as far as telling women he had no children. What an asshole! This man was never going to change; he didn't want to obviously. He wouldn't even take the time to see the boys he had with Anna. He never once fought for them.

Some men don't understand that their children can feel a lot of pain when they don't try hard enough to have their kids by their side. The excuse is always that they don't want to put them through all the battles. What they don't understand is that sometimes, a child is better off seeing how much love their father has, how he will fight to the end to have them in his life, even if it means calling the police or going to court. Without that effort, it can just make the child feel betrayed, especially if they are with another woman with children. It can make them feel hate, resentment, or even worthless if the other parent isn't a good parent. I wished my father had rescued my brothers and me.

Victoria was about to be two years old and started getting sick. She stopped breathing one evening and ended up at Driscoll Children's Hospital and was diagnosed with a respiratory virus. My poor baby was in quarantine and was so sick and miserable. After a week, she was released. I was so stressed out and tired, and I had had enough and decided to leave again.

When I told him I was leaving, he begged me to stay and told me he was in the process of getting us a house. He knew exactly what to say to get me to stay. Of course, I stayed again. The kids needed a home and their father. We moved into our new house, and it was different. He started staying home more often. We both worked, and my mother watched Frankie and Victoria at times. We met a couple of two houses down and got pretty close to them; they became our best friends. We never went out to clubs until we started hanging out with them. We would have so much fun, and we were really good at dancing together. We entered contests at times.

It was a blast until he started cheating on me again. I didn't know what to do. I had issues with my birth-control pills and found out I was pregnant again. We hardly even have sex. He was too busy with other women instead of his wife. All it took was one time with me, and boom, I was having another baby! It was so unexpected, and I freaked out. I had to tell someone, so I confided in my friend who lived two houses down. After all, they did know a lot about us, and we knew a lot about them. She told me that I had things good and to do the right thing. I ended up staying but decided I was going to start nursing school, finish, and then leave his ass, so I dealt with all the crap for a while.

CHAPTER NINE

An Untimely End

I took the kids to my mother's apartment one day to visit with her, and she was talking about getting together at the beach. Rocky had an injury to his foot and was limping around the apartment. A two-by-four piece of wood had fallen on his foot and caused it to swell up. My mother wasn't being too attentive and was frustrated with him. Remember, she had no patience. I really didn't want to go that day because it was too hot.

As my mother was driving out of the driveway and I was getting the kids ready to leave home, Rocky stood up and was trying to come at me. He took a few footsteps and just passed out and dropped to the ground. I ran outside and stopped my mother. She ran inside and yelled and was trying to pick him up. He came to, and she took him to the emergency room where they ended up admitting him. My mother was back and forth to the apartment that night. She told us he was awake and fine. When she went back to the hospital the following morning, she called us and told us he went into a coma. If he was talking like nothing had happened, why a coma? After all that, the following day, she told us he was diagnosed with gangrene. He had it on his foot where the two-by-four had hit him. It looked like a dead foot, almost like frostbite.

My mother was never told that they could cut off his foot so the gangrene wouldn't spread, and we didn't know about any infections like that. My mother left home to shower and change, and when she went back to the hospital, he was in a worse condition than before. We overheard the nurses and doctors talking as if they did something wrong. We were never informed of any incidents either. We didn't know what was going on. My mother didn't comprehend a lot of things the doctors were saying. I blew it off, and honestly, with everything that had happened to me and my brothers, I was hoping he wouldn't live. A few hours later, the gangrene had spread so fast it had reached his brain. He was on life support, and my mother was hoping for a miracle. She said people came out of comas all the time.

There we were, and the doctors told us the medicine they were giving him was the only thing keeping him alive. Every organ was already poisoned, including his brain. She was never told what could have been done to save him. They could have amputated his foot, and he would have had a chance to live, but everything happens for a reason. They just told my mother that eventually the medicine would stop working. As were sitting in the lobby, we heard code blue, and all the doctors and nurses ran to his room. My mother started screaming and crying and trying to go into the room. They had to call security to keep her from going in. Cold blue was yelled out five or six times, and they told my mom she needed to eventually sign the papers to remove the life support. She didn't want to, but the whole family was telling her she was just making him suffer. I was saying so many ugly things in my mind. I wanted him to suffer for all the things he did to me and my brothers. I wanted him gone. My mother signed the papers, and as they were removing all the machines he was hooked up to, they told us we could all go in as soon as they were done to pay our last respects. My mother began to worry about the funeral arrangements, and my family was trying to tell her not to think about it at that moment. It had just happened, and there was still a lot of time. Everyone mourned and stayed there for a while.

We all went home, and the first thing my mom did was turn to alcohol. My whole family was known to be very big drinkers, and it wasn't big news to anyone who knew the family. The whole family was there with my mother, helping her cope with the mourning of Rocky and talking about all the funny things he had done. I never saw these things or even heard anything funny about him. Why weren't they talking about all the bad things he had done—the drugs he did, all the alcohol, the abuse we experienced from him, the times he was always fighting? I overheard my aunt and mother talk about having a benefit for him to raise money for his funeral. They started the following day, asking his boss for help. Next thing I know, they had the money, and my mother had the dates for the coffin, rosary, and burial. She had the nerve to ask if I would give a speech during the rosary. Why would I give a speech about a man who did the things he did to me and my brothers? She asked me to speak of how he was there to take care of us more than my father.

"We had what we had because of him," she said.

That pissed me off. What I couldn't understand was how she could say that and think it was great to be in an efficiency apartment with a husband and three children. I never saw anyone doing more than the ordinary job to better our lives. I didn't even get pushed to go to school and have a career. Well, the funeral came and went, and I didn't really get to start speaking because I broke down and started crying in front of everyone, not because of his passing but because of what my mother asked me to do.

I remember my brothers walking up to me at the little altar where I was standing and putting their arms around me, and that just had me break down more. I couldn't talk; my chest started feeling tight. I started seeing a lot of the men walking out of the funeral home, and a lot of the women were crying. Everyone came up to us and paid their respects and asked if we were okay. I looked over to my brother Jerry, and I saw him crying and asked myself *why*. Was it because of how my mother was mourning? How she said nice things about Rocky? I got abused and raped by this monster, and I still felt so sad for my brothers and felt that they got the worst out of everything. The rosary was over, and everyone went back to the apartment and started drinking as usual with my mother and some of my aunts. They were cutting up some menudo to eat for the following day after the burial. The burial took place. Everyone went to my mother's apartment to eat, and they started drinking again and crying.

After that day, it was as if everyone just went about their business as if he never existed, except my mother. My brothers took care of her as she started drinking very heavily and going out. She was depressed for a while and chose to go down that route. She had had a few relationships, but they didn't work. It was either them or her. My mother was not an easy person to get along with. She was a very blunt person, and if you were around her, you would hear any negative things she didn't like, especially if they were about you.

PART FOUR

A Diamond in the Rough

A diamond doesn't start out polished and shining. It once was nothing special, but with enough pressure and time, becomes spectacular. I'm that diamond.

—Solange Nicole

CHAPTER TEN

Faceted Changes

My mother met this one man who turned out to be great and who treated her really good and was a hard worker. His name was Frank. My brothers got along with Frank, so I knew he was a good person. He persuaded my mother to move out of the Mohawk Apartments and into a four-apartment complex. We all moved into our own apartment in the same vicinity.

I had another daughter, and I finally left Max for good. He was too excited about being a bachelor and wasn't around much for the kids, so I had to do it on my own. It wasn't easy finishing up school and getting into the medical field full-time with three children, but I managed with some help. Things went great, and what I didn't accomplish in high school, I did easily in college. I graduated college with honors, and I got hired while doing my internship. It felt great! My life was going to be so different.

I loved my job; I loved getting up in the morning just to go to work. It was pretty hard having to maintain a family on my own with no help from their father. He just pretty much disappeared and only wanted to see the kids for an hour or so. Most of the time, he was just being nosy and wanted to see what was up with me. I didn't budge. I hated that bastard for the things he did to me. I really didn't care if he was in their life or not. I still had to do what I had to do to take care of my kids.

Max and his new wife (Mari, my ex-best friend) were having a good time; they were always out and were not worried about the kids. She divorced her husband, and six months later, she married Max. She told me she fell in love with him, and I basically told her she fell in love with his lies. She had two daughters he was always around with but never his own.

Things were okay and good for me and the kids. We had our own place and our own car, and my kids and I were able to go on trips from time to time. I would go out with my girlfriends when I had the chance to release some steam. I dated once in a blue moon, but I liked being on my own, not having to deal with a man. They were all the wrong ones. There was always something wrong and immature about them—things I didn't want to deal with. I eventually got into a couple of serious relationships after a while and remarried, but nothing turned out great with that marriage. It just turned out to be another divorce.

I got sick and was in and out of the hospital for a few months. They couldn't figure out what was wrong. One minute it could have been cancer, and the next minute I was told it was a hiatal hernia above the lining of my stomach. I couldn't hold down any food until we experimented with a few different drugs the doctor prescribed. It turned out to be something so easy that managed my hernia. Nexium and Pepcid administered together did it. Although, I would have to have surgery in the future if the hernia got too big. No doctor wanted to touch it due to how small it was at the moment. I have since then managed it greatly, and eating the right foods also helped. I decided to stay single for a while, moved out to another apartment, then finally had my own home. I traveled here and there and made lots of new friends. Life was good, and I decided to start my own business. I started my own cleaning service—Helly's Cleaning Services.

With some white printer paper and a Sharpie, my daughter and I decided to make some flyers to pass out around my neighborhood. The following day, I received a few phone calls, and one thing lead to another from there. I started off cleaning homes, which lead the women I worked with to talk to their friends about housekeeping. My phone number was passed around, and it brought me more work. Business was okay; I wasn't making much money, but it did help a lot. I was working at the School of Science and Technology. It was a good job, but I wanted to be my own boss and work my own hours. I was always looking for bigger and better things. It turned out to be a lot of work because I was working on my days off nonstop.

One of my customers owned a popular nightclub and gave my number to another owner. Eventually, I started cleaning auto dealerships. It was a lot more money than I was used to and helped beyond what I was making. It took a toll on me after two years. I still had my day job and cleaned these dealerships at night. I barely had any sleep. I had to keep going for the sake of my kids. I couldn't give up after all the hard work I put in. My daughter was heading to college, and my other daughter was still in high school. My son had his wife and my grandkids. I always had in my mind that I had to make up for lost time and do what I couldn't do for my kids in the past.

It felt good to start up a business and work my butt off. I was overwhelmed with all the dealerships and needed to quit my day job. It was a scary and risky feeling for me. I never had my own business and never was without a job since I was sixteen years old. So I did. I quit and hired a few employees who could help out with the dealerships. Not everyone worked out. My cousin Valerie ended up working out and being with me the longest. Things were great!

One day, I got a phone call from a good friend that a builder needed some help cleaning, doing makereadies. Makereadies are the final cleanups done after the home is built. It is a process done before the buyers move in. When I saw how fast this builder was building, I got excited. All I saw were dollar signs. It was as if when you own a business, you want more and more. Well, at least some of us. I took on the work, but I was too tired at times to check on the dealerships. Thank God for Valerie. The superintendent for this work ended up getting fired and started with another builder. He loved my work so much he called me and wanted me to start with his new builder, and I did. I had more work than ever.

I quit cleaning most of the dealerships and stayed with one. Valerie was a great and trustworthy employee, so I had no worries with her taking care of the dealership. While working on the makereadies, one of the builders came up to me and asked me to get rid of a trailer that was on one of his properties. It was full of trash, and he asked if I could go dump it and just keep the trailer. If I did that, he would let me start picking up all his trash inside and out as the homes were being built. I did my homework to figure out a price and was freaked out on the amount of money a person could make just picking up all the trash and materials at each property. I said yes to the builder. I didn't know how things would turn out with the dealership, but the owner, in particular, was looking into getting rid of me. I cleaned his home from time to time, and his wife didn't get along with the help very well. Nothing was ever good enough for her.

One day, I was called into the dealership and was told they had budget cuts and they no longer needed my services. I knew the real reason. The owner himself couldn't even tell me; he had the accountant do it for him. How unprofessional, but then again, I was known to stand up to men in high places, so maybe that was why. I had to train myself that way. Men in business always think us women don't know what we're talking about, or they think as if we can't get the job done. But as the saying goes, "Where one door closes, another opens." I was upset that day, but the excitement I had about the construction sites took over, so it didn't matter after that.

The work was hard, but I pushed myself to the limit and worked all day and late nights. I had to because of my bills and my kids. I had to keep going. I tried hiring a few people, but no one ever lasted too long. The job was hard. It was very hard to work while it was hot outside, and picking up leftover material from the new homes was heavy and could take a toll on the body big-time. I never really had dependable employees. I always had new people, but work was steady and good. Word got around on how good I was, and little by little, other builders started to call for my services. Our lives were becoming better for me and my kids. It felt good to be able to pay all my bills and still have plenty left to use on myself and my kids.

Then I had my accident. I was told this person hit me out of nowhere while on my way to work. It was a head-on collision, and she was speeding. They said she smelled like alcohol, but they never tested her. I'm guessing because she was an old woman. I was hurt pretty bad. Using a neck brace and crutches was a very hard thing to get used to. I had physical therapy every day. It was hard, and I didn't work for a bit. Thank God the builders and everyone at the construction sites understood and had my back. They saw how hard I worked, working like a man. Everyone told me work would be waiting for me, and I was very grateful for that. When I went back to work, I was still in crutches. All I did was drive. I had a few employees who did all the work, and they were great. These guys really took care of me.

I had to travel to Houston once a month for injection's in my spine. It felt good for a while, but it would always wear off before the month was up. I eventually had back surgery and was told my walking wouldn't be the same. I was told I would be limping. I couldn't accept that. I worked my legs out hard-core, and lifted weights when I could. I proved everyone wrong and started walking better after a few months. I had a case pending and had a lawsuit with the person who hit me. It took about two years until the case was over. I came into some money that was very useful to me and my family.

CHAPTER ELEVEN

A Polished Life

Today Frankie and Trista have my four beautiful grandbabies. My son is a first-respond rescuer. Trista just finished college and is doing hair. Victoria and Christian just had my grandson. She is still in college, and he is a firefighter. Emily and Jacob just had my granddaughter. She is a stay-at-home mother, and he work in the oil field industry. My daughters are both in the lives of their stepbrothers, Joseph and Anthony.

Their father still doesn't try to see or talk to them. I was told they want nothing to do with Max. Crazy how things end up. My mother since then has changed for the better. We visit at times, and I now get a better love from her compared to then. She has undergone triple bypass surgery recently and has recovered very well. She is a little more cautious about what she eats and respects life a lot more now. I forgave her for everything she did and didn't do, and our relationship has grown a lot stronger than before. To some, it may not seem as strong, but to me, it was a big step. We are taking it one day at a time.

I love my family very much, and I am happy to know they didn't experience the things I went through or chose to go down the wrong path. As for me, I finally have a great husband. Third time is a charm. He was under my nose the whole time.

Jesus Christ always has his timing, and its always right. He turned out to be a cousin of a friend. He asked me out on a date through Messenger so fast he didn't even give me a chance to get to know him, at least over the phone. He wanted to take me to dinner, which was on a Sunday, but I had my 5K that day. So we decided to go on Monday. His name is Michael. He wanted to try a place we both hadn't been to, so we decided on a new restaurant called the Ginger Café. I awaited for his arrival, and when he got to my house, he got down his truck to open my door. He was driving a huge truck with a lift, so assumed he would be tall. He was the same height as me and was very handsome. We got to the café and ordered our drinks, and they ended up screwing up on his drink. They added banana, and he literally hated it. It made him cringe; it was so funny.

He took me to a movie after dinner. I couldn't even remember what movie we watched. We were both so nervous. He was always red, and I was always laughing. As we walked out the theater, he asked me if I had to go home. I told him no, and he said he was going to kidnap me for the rest of the night. He took me to a bar called Izzy's. We played some games and drank a few beers. We talked for a long time, and then his kids called, so he needed to go home.

Michael had two children. Timmy was fourteen years old, and his daughter, Trish, was sixteen years old. They would stay with him and his mother from time to time. He ended up dropping me off, and we talked on the phone before bed for a bit. He said he wanted to see me again. It felt like high school again. Mornings were great for me. I would get up for work so happy and eager to read his text messages. He couldn't wait to see me after work either, so I would go home, shower, and get ready for him to pick me up. He would take me to dinner, shoot pool, or take walks and talk. He was the one for me; he was good to me. I wanted to see how the relationship would go.

I didn't want to be thinking of serious issues if things didn't work out. The day came that he had to leave town for work. He didn't go far, so it felt okay for me. On his birthday, I bought him a birthday card and had his kids, mother, and grandmother sign it. I drove to Victoria, Texas, and surprised him with it and the gifts I got him. He cried, and it made me feel so much compassion for him. A month later, he started wanting to drive back and forth to my apartment to see me more often. He said he was so happy to be with me and had a reason to come home besides coming home for the kids as well.

My birthday was here, and he showed up one morning after work with a bunch of balloons and a few gifts. It made my day! Things were perfect. There were little flaws, but who cares? It was the little things that any strong relationship could overcome. We talked and decided he would move into my apartment. Things were like nothing I had experienced before. Our kids were great, and our lives were great! We were both working, and on our days off, we would go out and have fun.

A few months later, I noticed he was always looking at engagement rings when we were inside stores, shopping. I never said anything, until one day, he asked for my opinion, and he literally ended up buying me the ring I wanted right at that moment. We were so excited that we ended up telling everyone and got together and had a few drinks.

Months went by, and his birthday was coming around again, so I bought him concert tickets as a surprise. I told him we were going to the beach to go hang out for the weekend just to relax, but right before we left for South Padre Island, we talked about eloping.

We went on a Friday morning and got our marriage license and decided when we would return back to Corpus Christi and that we would get married at the courthouse. We drove and had a great time in South Padre Island. We had a great room and good food. When I told him I had tickets, he freaked out. He was so excited. We rented a go-cart and stopped at a great restaurant, then we headed to the concert. We had a blast! We stayed in South Padre for three days and then drove back home. We were getting ready that Monday morning for the courthouse.

I had a simple off-white dress on, and he looked so handsome with his jeans and button-up off-white shirt. We were nervous but kept giggling as we said our I dos. We took a few pictures, had lunch, and literally went straight home to change and went to work. We had the construction company and now a tile business, and he still kept up with the welding. We were a pretty busy couple at the time.

All of my life's experiences had added great value to my life, but this one to me was just as big as when I had my kids. I was once broken in spirit and lost, but I worked very hard to put myself together, my children, and my business. The only thing that was missing at the time was my husband, and the Lord sent him to me. And after all the things I had been through, I turned out to be the person who I was meant to be—the person who finally has a great husband by my side, great kids who have done great things, and a family full of love. Everything else was a bonus.

For I know the plans I have for you…plans to prosper you and not to harm you, plans to give you hope and a future.

—Jeremiah 29:11

ABOUT THE AUTHOR

From an abusive household to failed relationships, Angelica Galbraith has become a former owner of a small business to an owner of a few companies and has recently been able to retire. She is married with three children, two stepchildren, and six grandchildren. She has since been traveling alongside her wonderful husband and writing out of hotel rooms every moment she can. Her accomplishments have also included being a cosmetologist, nurse, cook, construction worker/owner; and she is on the verge of building an online business. She is a jack-of-all-trades. She has also managed to have time to train herself into being a healthier person who practices weight training. Living by her motto "My life isn't over until I say it's over," Angelica has been provided with many experiences and opportunities in her life that proved she is always destined for success.